52-Week Devotional
for Christian Women

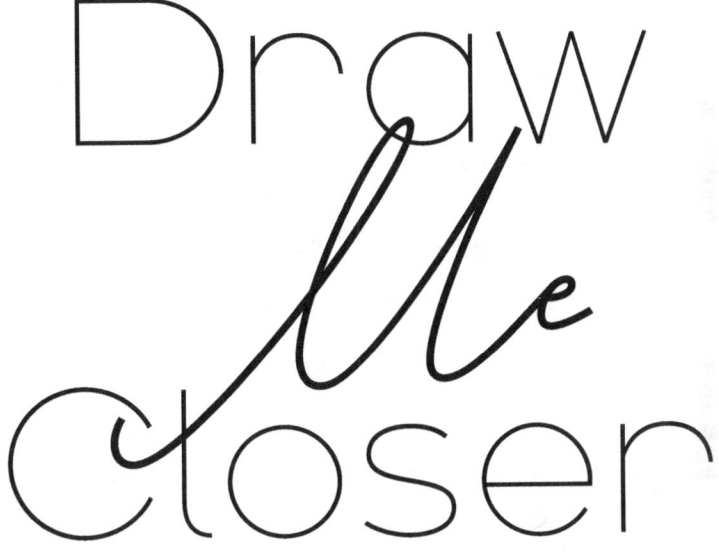

Draw Me Closer

THE 4 PILLARS OF GROWTH

By JOSEPHINE THOMAS

Kingdom Assignment for Christian Women

Jesus spoke of perils, times that will confront believers in the "last days."

It appears these days are here and a lot has been unleashed upon the world and the children of God. In light of this prediction of woes, the Lord asks in Luke 18:8, when the "The Son of Man" returns, will he find faith on the earth? However, the mercy of God has released help like this devotional to assist believers, especially women, to keep the light and will of God burning in their hearts.

This devotional opens our eyes of understanding, to discern our true identity in God. That we were created in the image and likeness of God. Designed to grow in the wisdom and knowledge of Him and to mature and fly as "eagles." Not bound like chickens.

This devotional is absolutely essential to have and be kept for regular study and meditation on the word of God. This book will help us learn to take responsibility for our Father's estate—the earth.

Thus, we will ensure God's kingdom comes on earth as it is in heaven (Matthew 6:10).

~ *Pastor Patience Dowuona Hammond*

This devotional book is God's recipe for the needs of His people—especially for those whose conditions are reflected by "The Daughter of Abraham," whom Jesus "saw," "touched," and "healed" (Luke 13: 10–17). It is a timely, practical and simple—yet a very profound work, *"for such a time as this."* It serves as a "weekly tonic" for those who follow the author's prescriptions. The book is also encouraging, comforting and reassuring, knowing that: We are created in God's image; God's plan for us is for our good—always; and that God can be trusted in every trying situation. It is highly recommended as God's answer to our prayers, in these tough and discouraging seasons.

~ *Dr. Goodluck Akhabue Christopher*

In response to God's calling, Evangelist Josephine Thomas has a natural empathy and passion for helping people know God better and serve Him more intentionally.

An excellent short book and a much-needed devotional: "Draw Me Closer" covers essential elements of Christian growth. It is both simple and clear. We found it to be instructive, stimulating and helpful, taking the reader through the lens to the heart of the Gospel!

As you read this devotional, it is our prayer you will be inspired and challenged to a deeper walk with the Lord.

~ Anthony & Sarah Thomas
Overseer and First Lady-Pastor – FT Church

Draw Me Closer: The Four Pillars of Growth is a powerful and transformative devotional for any woman longing for a deeper relationship with God. Josephine Thomas has beautifully woven together scripture, reflection, and prayer, creating a sacred space for personal growth and spiritual renewal. Each week, the carefully crafted questions invite the Holy Spirit's revelation, encouraging readers to pause, reflect, and hear God's voice in new and profound ways.

This devotional is more than just words on a page—it's a journey of healing, wholeness, and restoration. Josephine speaks from experience, and her wisdom and encouragement resonate deeply. She understands the struggles of faith, the longing for clarity, and the desire to walk boldly in purpose.

If you are seeking empowerment, insight, and a deeper connection with God, this devotional will be a life-changing companion on your faith journey. It will challenge you, inspire you, and most importantly— draw you closer to the heart of God. I wholeheartedly recommend Draw Me Closer to every woman ready to embrace her Kingdom identity and step into a new season of spiritual growth.

~ Kelly Williams Hale
Speaker, Author, and Mentor

Draw Me Closer: The Four Pillars of Growth
52-Week Devotional for Christian Women

@ 2025 Josephine Thomas. All rights reserved.

Published by Pure and Unblemished Limited

ISBN: 979-8-9921054-3-8

All Scriptures are from the New Living Translation Bible unless otherwise stated.

Scripture quotations are taken from the Holy Bible, New Living Translation, copyright © 1996, 2004, 2015 by Tyndale House Foundation. Used by permission of Tyndale House Publishers, Inc., Carol Stream, Illinois 60188. All rights reserved.

Cover design and formatting @ 2025 by Kelly Williams Hale

Dedication

I dedicate this book to my extraordinary husband, Emile, and to my precious daughters, Patience and Deborah. When life hit me hard, you stood with me. We held hands together in prayer and intercession, drawing closer to God. The enemy came against me so I might fall, but you stood with me, encouraging me to keep going and not quit. The consistency of your kindness and support has been a great help to me during that season. Thank you for your love and care for me. You stood together and took specific responsibilities from me so I could focus on this assignment from God. This book happened because you were the helpers God assigned to me. I thank God for you. May God reward you bountifully in Jesus' Name.

To my spiritual mother, mother and mentor, Pastor Patience Dowuona Hammond. You are the embodiment of a Proverbs 31 woman. Devoted, full of virtue, wisdom, and faith in God. Thank you for holding my hands in good and hard times. Thank you for mentoring me. Thank you for your prayers and intercession for me. Thank you for laughing and crying with me. Thank you for the good counsel and encouragement. Thank you for helping me stay close to God despite life's challenges. Mothers like you are rare to find. God bless you richly and return to you 100-fold your goodness towards me in Jesus' Name.

To my dearest sister in Christ, Tracy Renaud. Your heart towards me is so pure. You have encouraged me to forget the past and press forward in God. You have constantly reminded me that I have so much in me and that I should stand for God's calling. You inspired me and stood with me to do what God has called me to do. You are a great delight and joy to me, and I am confident you have my back. You have supported and helped me overcome my life challenges; a friend who loves always. You demonstrate all attributes of the fruits of the Spirit, and are a true woman of God. Thank you for being there for me and all your prayers and intercession for me. May God bless you for all the goodness you have shown me and more in Jesus' Name.

Acknowledgements

My uttermost gratitude to Yahweh—my LORD, and Jesus Christ, and the Holy Spirit, my helper, shield, deliverer, and glory. My eyes are consistently lifted to Him in awe of his goodness and love towards me. He gave me this book through the Holy Spirit and made it possible for it to be born to many women of God. Thank you, Abba Father, that this precious book will be a blessing to many women of God worldwide. As each woman of God enters their Sacred Place, they will establish a relationship with you, find their purpose on earth, and impact others for your kingdom. *"May your Kingdom come soon. May your will be done on earth, as it is in heaven"* (Matthew 6:10).

God's will for you
flows from abiding
in the Sacred Place.

Pillar One: Relationship with God

Drawing Closer to God,
Know His Attributes.

Pillar Two: Spiritual Growth

True Fulfillment in the Sacred Place With God,
Know Who You Are.

Pillar Three: Personal Growth

Encouragement for Self-Development,
Persevere Through the Journey.

Pillar Four: Purpose

Discover and Fulfill Your God-Given Purpose,
Utilize the Giftings Within.

Table of Contents

PILLAR TWO: SPIRITUAL GROWTH

PILLAR THREE: PERSONAL GROWTH

Introduction

This 52-week devotional book aims to help you know God better, build a stronger relationship with Him, be grounded in your faith, and motivate you to spend time in His presence.

Why is it called *Draw Me Closer: The Four Pillars of Growth?*

Firstly, drawing closer to God enables you to have a more intimate relationship with Him. Knowing the attributes of God's nature will support you in difficult times that arise in your life. You will be able to trust and hold on, knowing who God is.

Secondly, imagine a structured building with four pillars. Each pillar is required to sustain the integrity of the building. The four pillars selected for this devotional are:

- *Relationship with God*
- *Spiritual Growth*
- *Personal Growth*
- *Purpose*

Pillar One: Relationship with God

By knowing Him more deeply, you strengthen this relationship and learn to trust and love Him more.

Pillar Two: Spiritual Growth

Spiritual growth helps you know who you are and enables you to grow your faith while learning to pray, fight, and stand.

Pillar Three: Personal Growth

Personally, when adversity comes to confront and shake you, this is where remembering who you are—while holding onto God's promises for your life—will get you through.

Pillar Four: Purpose

The last pillar is *Purpose*. Through your relationship with God—as you draw closer to Him through the journey—you will discover God's will and be able to fulfill His purpose for your life. You have a great calling from God within you right now. All you need to do is find out what that purpose is then embrace it with all your heart. You can live a life of contentment and fulfillment.

Never be afraid to pray and talk to God about anything. Ask away! Just know He loves you so much. He died on the cross for your sins and the sins of all the world. He will always be attentive to you. Give God a chance to be the leader of your life and watch as He makes everything new. This devotional will provide a good foundation, encouragement, and the discipline to take with you throughout your life.

How to Use This Book

This 52-week devotional book contains scriptures, messages, and reflection questions. You will need a journal, diary, pen, bible, and quiet place. The devotional's goal is to encourage and strengthen your relationship for growth with God every week of the year. The idea is to reflect on each week's scripture, meditate on it, let God reveal insight, and talk to Him about your discoveries. He loves to hear from you.

Write down what God reveals to you personally in your Sacred Place. There is a short prayer at the end of each week's message. You can use it or feel free to use your own words to pray and express your heart to God.

Woman of God Message

Woman of God, you may have experienced heavy storms in life which brought fierce winds from the enemy through words of discouragement or calamity. I write this book to bless you. I want you to draw closer to God and strengthen your relationship with Him to discover the God-given purpose for your life.

My heart's cry for you is that you are encouraged to draw nearer to the presence of God daily through this devotional and throughout your life. Stay on His pathway. See your limitations and the limitations placed upon you by others broken off. Refuse to bow to the negative voices of the enemy. Be determined. Defy the odds. Tell yourself *"I can do this with the help of Almighty God."* Start now, change your destiny, and change your life. Focus on—and hold on—to God's words and promises throughout this devotional.

Woman of God, nothing is impossible for God. Your breakthroughs are closer than you think. I am with you and cheering you along to succeed. But more importantly, the great *I Am Who I Am* is with you every step of the way. Do not lose heart. Move forward with courage and boldness.

Blessings,

Josephine Thomas

Author and Fellow Woman of God

Pillar One:

Relationship With God

Drawing Closer to God, Know His Attributes.

"Intimacy is Born from the Secret Place Draw Closer to God."

Creator God

Scripture:

> *You alone are the LORD. You made the skies and the*
> *heavens and all the stars. You made the earth and the*
> *seas and everything in them. You preserve them all,*
> *and the angels of heaven worship you.*
>
> ~ Nehemiah 9:6 NLT

Woman of God:

Are you ever surprised at the wondrous works of God or enraptured by His craftsmanship and intricacy for detail? From the creation of people, birds, and animals to the designs of nature and the vast seas, to the dreamy sunsets or even shooting stars, God created them so you can enjoy His tangible handiwork here on earth. Scripture tells you not only did God create all things but that God preserves them as well. When you look at the word preserve, you can visualise the nature of God as a guardian, defender, protector, rescuer, deliverer, redeemer, and keeper. No wonder it says that the angels worship God. When God finished creating everything, He said it was good. He did not leave creation to fend for itself. God will always be the creation champion. He created all things for His good pleasure, of which extraordinary you are included. Never forget or let anyone make you feel less than or even suggest that you are a mistake. God thought about you; He knew you, designed you, and provided all you need. Might this be worth worshiping and giving God a shout of praise for? Never forget God called forth something from nothing and brought forth life. Let God create something new and wonderful for you and in you because He genuinely cares for you. This week, intentionally reflect on God's wondrous creation. See what you notice and give God thanks and praise for it.

Reflection Questions:

- What amazes or excites you when thinking about God's creation?

- Do you have childlike awe for your Creator God?

- Do you include yourself when thinking about the splendor of God's creation?

Prayer:

Dear God, thank you for being the God of creation and for creating me. Thank you for my life. Forgive me when I take your handiwork for granted. Forgive me for not seeing your wonderful works with awe. Please help me to appreciate you and all you do for me every day, in Jesus' name, Amen.

Covenant-Keeping God

Scripture:

> *"Now if you will obey me and keep my covenant,*
> *you will be my own special treasure from among all*
> *the peoples on earth; for all the earth belongs to me.*
> *And you will be my kingdom of priests, my holy nation."*
> *This is the message you must give the people of Israel.*
>
> ~ Exodus 19:5-6 NLT

Woman of God:

A covenant is a promise or an agreement between two people or a group of people; like a marriage—a covenant agreement to share a monogamous relationship forsaking all others—which is legally binding. Unfortunately, this can change if either party does not correctly adhere to the terms and conditions. God's covenant is different as His terms and conditions are non-negotiable. There is obedience and acceptance when entering into agreement; the terms and conditions of God's covenant are unchanging. The old covenant in scripture was a written law on a stone tablet and refers to this agreement, set up on Mount Sinai. Let's face it: Moses had a lot of people under his charge so God gave him a framework for governance, conduct, and right living. The law came with many ceremonial rituals, including one for the transgression of sin. Each year, the appointed high priest entered the Tabernacle of God and poured out the blood of the sacrificed animal for the sins of the people. But this law and blood could not remove the stain of the sin of death. It was a temporary intervention. God would not let anything stand in the way of separation from His people, separation from you. God would make a way and a plan for you to have life. Notably, this covenant foreshadowed a new one, producing life once and for all. This week, reflect on God's unchanging covenant for you and how it differs from your other covenants.

Reflection Questions:

- What are your thoughts on a covenant-keeping God?

- What do you think about your covenant being one of life and not separation?

- How do you feel about all God has done for you?

Prayer:

Dear God, thank you for Jesus and His Blood shed for me. Thank you for granting me life and not leaving me in the darkness. Thank you for your Holy Spirit, who is life. Please help me to live a life pleasing to you, in Jesus' name, Amen.

Holy, holy, holy

Scripture:

*Each of these living beings had six wings, and their wings
were covered all over with eyes, inside and out.
Day after day and night after night, they keep on saying,
"Holy, holy, holy is the Lord God, the Almighty—the one
who always was, who is, and who is still to come."*

~ Revelation 4:8 NLT

Woman of God:

Holiness is God's Divine, pure, intrinsic nature. The four living, six-winged creatures said continually *"Holy,"* flying back and forth, day and night, never ceasing, forever declaring this. These living creatures had eyes everywhere, declaring God's Holiness wherever they were. Their creation was for this specific purpose, to fulfill this one task. Can you imagine this beautiful picture? How about thinking about this: God, who created these incredible creatures, also created you for a specific purpose. Like these creatures, holiness is a requirement, whereby you become morally transformed in the likeness of God. For the Scriptures say, *"You must be holy for I am holy"* (1 Peter 1:16). How do you become holy, you ask? Scripture says, *"Make them holy by the truth; teach them your word, which is truth*" (John 17:17). As you read the Word, understand who God is, spend time with Him, and build a strong relationship, you begin the process to transforming to the holiness of God. Eventually, your relationship will produce clarity and fulfillment of your purpose. You, too, can declare God's goodness and that God is Holy, holy, holy. This week, reflect on God's Holiness. Think about how these creatures say "*Holy*" three times, continually.

Reflection Questions:

- What does God's Holiness mean to you?

- Knowing the truth of the Word makes you holy. How is your engagement with the Word?

- What might you do differently to improve your relationship with God?

Prayer:

Dear God, thank you for enabling me to become more like you each day through your Word. Forgive me when I do not spend enough time with you or in your Word. Forgive me for any hindrances contrary to your holiness that would keep us apart and please help me release them to you. Please transform every area of my life by your Word, in Jesus' name, Amen.

I Am Who I Am

Scripture:

But Moses protested, "If I go to the people of Israel and tell them, 'The God of your ancestors has sent me to you,' they will ask me, 'What is his name?' Then what should I tell them?" God replied to Moses, "I AM WHO I AM. Say this to the people of Israel: I AM has sent me to you."

~ Exodus 3:13-14 NLT

Woman of God:

The scripture above says Moses was protesting to the God of heaven. Moses enquired about God's name for his assignment and God replied, "tell them, *I AM WHO I AM.*" What a response! Interestingly, God has no shortage of names in the bible. However, this is God's most Holy, revered, and sacred name. *I AM WHO I AM* means Yahweh and, in English, translates as "LORD." Do you get a sense of what God was saying here? God declared *I AM* the one who was, who is, and who will be. *I AM* the one who always existed before the beginning; the Alpha and Omega. Names are significant for the Israelites. Abraham was the father of nations and Jesus is the promised Saviour. Moses' name reflected his harrowing beginning in life; saved from the water. His mother's name, Jochebed, means Yahweh is my glory. Have you ever wondered—with all the names of God—He chose for you to personally call Him by His most holy, pure, and sacred name? The great *I AM WHO I AM* has introduced Himself to you. Remember, you know God's name. So whatever you are going through today, you can know there is one you can call upon: the great *I AM WHO I AM*. He will hear you and speak to you about whatever you are going through. This week, reflect on how you know God's most sacred name.

Reflection Questions:

- What does it mean for you to know God's name?

- What does your name mean? Does it tell a story about who you are?

- Do you have difficulty talking to God through adversity? How might you change that?

Prayer:

Dear God, thank you for being the great I AM WHO I AM. Thank you that I can call upon your name at any time, whether in good times or in times of trouble. Forgive me when I forget who you are and all you do for me. Please help me turn to you—first—for your strength and solution, instead of being exhausted alone, in Jesus' name, Amen.

The Messiah Son

Scripture:

> *Simon Peter answered, "You are the Messiah,*
> *the Son of the living God."*
>
> ~ Matthew 16:16 NLT

Woman of God:

In this scripture, you read God's revelation to Simon Peter about who Jesus was. Some translations say *Christ,* which means the anointed one. Jesus is also the *Son of the living God,* and no one else can boast that title. Jesus was anointed and appointed to do the most remarkable redemptive work ever accomplished upon this earth. Only He could do it! These are just a few names referring to Jesus: The Son of the living God, The Saviour, a Prophet, a High Priest, and a King. Jesus had an assignment on earth as seen in John 3:16-17, *"For this is how God loved the world: He gave his one and only Son, so that everyone who believes in him will not perish but have eternal life. For God sent his Son into the world not to judge the world, but to save the world through him."* This redemptive work led to death on the cross for humanity's sins. Jesus came to do the will of God out of love for you, to save you from an eternal damnation of separation. The Son of the living God—Jesus—

came all this way just for you. He did not dodge or shake off that responsibility and most would have said, "Forget this," and gone about their business. But not God. He deemed you worthy of this sacrificial ransom. Hopefully, that will uplift your spirit with whatever you are facing today. Know God has an unfailing love that is immeasurable and He went to such lengths to have a relationship with you. Reflect on God's sacrificial love for you this week.

Reflection Questions:

- What do you think about the sacrificial love of God for you?

- Have you called upon the living God today?

- What names signify who God is for you?

Prayer:

Dear God, thank you for Jesus the Messiah and His selfless sacrifice for me. Forgive me for all my sins and wrongdoings. Please help me to live for you and your Kingdom assignment for my life. Thank you for being the true living God. Please help me understand the depths of your love, in Jesus' name, Amen.

The Holy Spirit of God

Scripture:

*But when the Father sends the Advocate as my representative—
that is, the Holy Spirit—he will teach you everything
and will remind you of everything I have told you.*

~ John 14:26 NLT

Woman of God:

The great God you serve is a Trinity, three in one: The Father, The Son, and The Holy Spirit. The Holy Spirit is the third person of the Trinity, and HE is co-eternal and co-equal. Do you wonder if the disciples were overjoyed knowing they would not be alone? Jesus would send another, the Spirit of the living God—the Holy Spirit—to dwell within you as Comforter, Helper, Advocate, Mediator, and Friend. He is the One who will lead you into all truth. An excellent provision of God not leaving you comfortless or friendless is that He sent His Holy Spirit to be with you. Hold on to this truth and reality—especially when you feel lonely—and remind yourself that you are not alone. Remember, you have a friend that sticks closer than a brother. When you need comfort because you feel fragile, He places around you His arms to support you best. God said He will never leave or forsake you; he is an ever-present God. The Holy Spirit longs to have a deeper relationship with you and help you fully know Jesus. Whatever happens in your relationships or environment, you serve a God who has provided for you in every way and His Holy Spirit abides within you. Take the time to get to know the Holy Spirit of God. He is right there with you. This week, reflect on the third person of the Trinity, the Holy Spirit.

Reflection Questions:

- What does your relationship with the Holy Spirit look like?

- Do you know the Holy Spirit as Comforter or Friend?

- Do you trust the leading of the Holy Spirit?

Prayer:

Dear God, thank you for your love and provision. Thank you for not leaving me alone and friendless. Thank you for sending your Holy Spirit to dwell in me and for His leading and guiding me into all truth to know Jesus more. Holy Spirit, please forgive me if I do not know you as well as I should. Please help me to know you better, in Jesus' name, Amen.

The Source of Love is God

Scripture:

> *We know how much God loves us, and we have put our trust in his love. God is love, and all who live in love live in God, and God lives in them.*
>
> ~ 1 John 4:16 NLT

Woman of God:

You may have heard that God is love. Clearly, this scripture shows that God truly is. God has many attributes of His nature, as mentioned throughout the Bible. Attributes like God is Holy, God is Faithful, God is Righteous, God is Love. Just ponder this: God is the source of love. He first loved you and no other can glory in this truth. Here are a few types of love. Familial love is for your family and is called *Storge*. Romantic and sensual love is called *Eros,* between husband and wife. A deep friendship love is called *Philia*, likened to David and Jonathan or Ruth and Noami. The love of God is the highest of all, called *Agape*. This type of love is unconditional, obedient, and sacrificial. God's love trumps all the other type of "love." God demonstrated this love through Jesus' blood sacrifice for the world's sins. His obedience led to death upon a cross to secure your love. God's love is so rich and compassionate that it can heal and transform you and your understanding. Even more incredible, you do not need to do anything to work it up or agitate it to get results. God is the source of love. All you need to do is connect with God and His love. Love only wants to love. As mentioned in the commandment, you have a call to love others. This week, reflect on whether you actively share the love of God with others.

Reflection Questions:

- What do you think about when reflecting on God's love?

- Have you connected with God's love today?

- Can you bring to God today any area of your life that needs healing and transforming by His love?

Prayer:

Dear God, thank you for being the source of love and loving
me. Thank you for your love—which is unfailing—and
that I can have confidence in your love for me and others.
Forgive me when I have placed other kinds of love above You.
Forgive me for not displaying your love to others in the right way.
Please help me change my imperfections to love better.
Please help me to be immersed in your love so I will always
be complete, in Jesus' name, Amen.

The Just and Righteous God

Scripture:

*He is the Rock; his deeds are perfect. Everything
he does is just and fair. He is a faithful God who
does no wrong; how just and upright he is!*

~ Deuteronomy 32:4 NLT

Woman of God:

This scripture gives you beautiful imagery of calling God a rock with perfect deeds. It shows strength, dependability, and fairness in all His ways. God is Holy, God is Truth, and God is Light. There is no sin in God, no darkness, and He does not lie. God presides over creation in a just and righteous manner, which is His nature. God loves justice and hates injustice and falsehood. He is upright in all His ways, fights for the weak and oppressed, and champions the voiceless and downtrodden. Maybe this is a place you are familiar with right now. The scripture says God is faithful and will always fight to bring about any injustice or unfairness in your life. So, hang on. God will vindicate you and the situation. Also, this is twofold. As image bearers of God, this is how you are to respond in this world. You, too, must fight the good fight against injustice, whether by championing a cause or helping orphans or widows or the broken-hearted. Just know you can make a difference in this world which could bring about a lasting change for the good of others. God does not take this responsibility lightly. One day God will have to judge the unjust rightly. They cannot go unpunished before an upright and fair God. He is faithful to His word and to you. This week, reflect on a faithful, just, and fair God working on your behalf.

Reflection Questions:

- What are your thoughts about God's nature being just and fair?

- Do you recognize God's hand of justice in your life?

- What are your thoughts about championing a cause?
  Do you have one?

Prayer:

Dear God, thank you for being upright in all your ways and fighting for me even when I don't see it. Forgive me when I have been slow or indifferent to responding to injustice. Please help me to be an actual image bearer of your love, justice, and righteousness. Please help me to have a voice for the voiceless and a heart for the downtrodden like yours, in Jesus' name, Amen.

The Sovereign God

Scripture:

For the LORD your God is the God of gods and Lord of lords.
He is the great God, the mighty and awesome God,
who shows no partiality and cannot be bribed.

~ Deuteronomy 10:17 NLT

Woman of God:

This scripture highlights God's sovereignty and clearly shows God's supremacy over everyone. There is none like God, in majesty and splendor or power and presence, and none can compare to God. He alone is the one true living God. No other God reigns over creation and the universe. God has ultimate control, power, and authority. Consider the magistrates or rulers on earth who may pass rulings or set legislation, yet none of them can dictate or pass laws over the authority of God. God does not show bias or partiality from one to another. He is fair in all His ways, unlike earthly officials who may take a bribe to sway decisions or motions in favour of opposing parties. God is an incorruptible, just, and righteous God who others cannot influence. You can rejoice that He is LORD, far above the rest. His nature is holy, mighty, unfailing love, just, and sovereign. God holds all things in correct balance without wavering or needing counsel from anyone. God is uniquely divine. There is no other like God to compare with because no one can compare to God. This week, reflect on God's sovereignty and how none other compares to the God you serve.

Reflection Questions:

- Have you placed anything above the sovereignty of God?

- What are your thoughts about God being incorruptible?

- Can you readily take your concerns to God now, knowing He is above all?

Prayer:

Dear God, thank you for being sovereign above every other God, all circumstances, and all powers and principalities. Thank you that no one can compare to you and I can serve the one true living God. Forgive me if I have placed anything above you through my misunderstanding. Thank you for being my God, in Jesus' name, Amen.

The Omniscient God

Scripture:

Remember the things I have done in the past.
For I alone am God! I am God, and there is none
like me. Only I can tell you the future before
it happens. Everything I plan will come to
pass, for I do whatever I wish.

~ Isaiah 46:9-10 NLT

Woman of God:

Do you ever have days in your life that seem complex and challenging? Those days when you cannot determine the forest for the trees, where everything appears obscure and difficult. Such days can be pretty common on the journey through life and you do not travel these paths alone. God knows the beginning from the end and everything in between. He sees the whole picture because He is the omniscient God, which means He is all-knowing. He knows everything you are going through, from yesterday to today and tomorrow. You may fret that you cannot focus on one singular tree, but God sees the entire forest, the streams, valleys, mountains, and any obstacles beyond. God knows your future. Even when your vision may be blurred and a trip to the optician is needed. Remind yourself that God knows. Not only that, but stir yourself up with what He has accomplished for you in the past, as the scripture says. Remind yourself who God is and His magnificence. God has planned everything according to His will and wishes. Today, try forgetting about the tree for a moment. Re-focus and keep your attention on the God who knows everything! This week, reflect on God knowing the whole picture of your life.

Reflection Questions:

- How often do you lose focus? What helps you re-focus on God?

- How do you imagine your future?

- Do you reflect on what God has done for you in your life?

Prayer:

Dear God, thank you for reminding me that you know everything. Therefore, I need not worry or fret. Forgive me when I spend time preoccupied with my circumstances and situation. Please help me remain focused on you this week and remind myself of all the wonderful things you have done for me. Please help me by giving you anything worrying me, in Jesus' name, Amen.

The Immutability of God

Scripture:

I am the LORD, and I do not change. That is why you descendants of Jacob are not already destroyed.

~ Malachi 3:6 NLT

Woman of God:

Change is an inevitable part of living. For instance, technology races along, ever-changing into the new. However, it pulls at your purse strings with an incessant need to continually upgrade to the latest systems and new models to keep relevant. Nonetheless, one thing will never change: God. He is unchanging, known as the *Immutability of God*, as shown in Hebrews 13:8 which says: *Jesus Christ is the same yesterday, today, and for ever.* That's extraordinary! Can you recall how many times you went back and forth regarding issues in life when you were uncertain about what to do? Conversely, God does not say one thing today and then something different tomorrow. God does not fluctuate with emotions or circumstances. God is unchanging. This shows that God's promises over you and your life remain unchanged. His promises of love for you. His hope for you. His best eternal plan for you. His success for you and every promise over you will stand.

The downside for the unrighteous means God's hatred for sin—and every word spoken regarding wickedness and riotous living—will also remain. God has such a heartfelt cry for the lost, and they need to be transformed by the unchanging Word. God's word will never pass away. But you can take hope this week that God is unchanging towards you. Hold onto every blessed promise knowing that God will not change His mind concerning you. This week, reflect on which areas of your life you need to remember God's unchanging promises.

Reflection Questions:

- What are your thoughts about the Immutability of God?

- What promises do you want to keep hold of with this assurance?

- Have you ever considered how the Immutability of God would impact others?

Prayer:

Dear God, thank you for never changing and that every promise over me will stand and come to pass. Thank you for watching over your Word and fulfilling it in my life. Please help me to keep hold of the promises when I face difficult times. Forgive me when I forget. Please help me in all that I do, in Jesus' name, Amen.

The Unfailing Love of God

Scripture:

*With your unfailing love you lead the people
you have redeemed. In your might,
you guide them to our sacred home.*

~ Exodus 15:13 NLT

Woman of God:

Earlier, you saw God as the source of love. Yet there is still more. God's love is also *unfailing*. Take a moment to think about that. A love that cannot fail. Often, people can claim to love you. However, their love does not come up to par—as we say here in England. They may abuse you, hurt, harm, intimidate, or even place demands on you and call it love. God's love requires nothing from you, which is very different. God loves you because He is the source of love and His love never fails. You can see this through the life of Jesus and what He accomplished for you. If failure had occurred, then the assignment on His life would have ended with no good news. But that is not how Jesus' story went. God's unfailing love filled Him. God's love is perfect, pure, unfailing, never-ending, forever giving, loving, and so much more. Be mindful of the love of God for you today. It is freely available for you. If you need it then receive it. Spend time today drinking in the love of God and stay as long as you like. God wants you to take all that you need. This week, reflect on God's unfailing love for you.

Reflection Questions:

- What are your thoughts on God's unfailing love?

- Can you recognise that you are loved?

- Can you put your trust in God's love for you?

Prayer:

Dear God, thank you for reminding me of your unfailing love that will never fail. Thank you Jesus, for accomplishing all you did for me. Forgive me when I have been too busy or stuck in my little world to acknowledge your presence. Thank you for your loving kindness towards me and those I love. Thank you for your love. I breathe in your love for me today and ask you to fill me to overflowing, in Jesus' name, Amen.

Shelter of God

Scripture:

*Those who live in the shelter of the Most High will find rest
in the shadow of the Almighty. This I declare about the LORD:
He alone is my refuge, my place of safety; he is my God,
and I trust him. For he will rescue you from every trap
and protect you from deadly disease. He will cover you
with his feathers. He will shelter you with his wings.
His faithful promises are your armour and protection.*

~ Psalm 91:1-4 NLT

Woman of God:

When the orchard of life supplies apples, you can produce apple pie. Yum! When you carry around lots of issues in life, your journey may feel quite weighty; producing chinks in your armour. You may have the impression of being under, instead of on top of, your predicament. A good opportunity would be to take shelter and refuge in the Most High. Here you will find peace and rest from your crisis. Imagine this beautiful picture of God as a bird of prey spreading enormous wings around you, lovingly embracing you. Keeping you safe from outside influences, whatever that may look like for you presently.

God is a place of refuge and safety. His loving arms long to hold you to keep you close and protected. Here, you can refresh yourself and gather your wits, especially when circumstances or the enemy keeps bombarding you with turmoil and chaos. You can rest in the peace, comfort, and safety of God. Release all the things you were carrying. Give them to God and let them fall off. Even if it is hard for you, trust God with what matters to you. He cares for you. If you need a place of safety and refuge this week, remember God's loving arms are open wide for you. Just run into them and He will receive you. This week, reflect on God as your refuge and shelter.

Reflection Questions:

- What are your thoughts on dwelling in the shadow of Almighty God?

- When did you last run into God's embracing arms? What happened?

- Where do you usually go—or what do you usually do—for refuge?

Prayer:

Dear God, thank you for providing for my every need. Forgive me when I try to handle situations on my own without you. Please help me trust you and run towards you, not from you. Please help me to know there is no more extraordinary place of safety for me than with you, the one who truly cares about me. Thank you, in Jesus' name, Amen.

God Reigns Forever

Scripture:

*You will bring them in and plant them on your
own mountain—the place, O LORD, reserved for your
own dwelling, the sanctuary, O LORD, that your hands
have established. "The LORD will reign for ever and ever!"*

~ Exodus 15:17-18 NLT

Woman of God:

God's reign is forever and ever. The Israelites had some tough
lessons to learn. They had a rough time, possibly wondering if they
would escape the cruelty of bondage and hardship with an enemy close
on their heels. Yet their old Egyptian adversary drowned before their eyes;
washed away by the Red Sea and delivered by the mighty hand of God.
They, too, would need to learn this truth about God, which says, "*The
LORD will reign forever and ever!*" What an amazing God to deliver in
such a miraculous way. Even more remarkable is His reign is forever with
no ending. Were the Israelites more enthralled by God's incredible
parting of the Red Sea or awed with the truth about their God? God's
hand moved on their behalf. His reign is forever and ever and will
never end. Wow! God wants to draw you close to Him, and what He

establishes, He will bring to pass. And even though it may take some time to understand this, do not worry because you are His. He wants you exactly where you are. You will have a lifetime to discover how excellent the LORD God is. So, no matter what is going on in your life this week, His words will remain established. He reigns forever. This week, reflect on all God has brought you through and the lessons you learned.

Reflection Questions:

- What caught your attention in today's message?

- Have you spent time with the truth that the LORD shall reign forever and ever? What does it mean for you?

- What might you do to be planted on God's mountain and established in His ways?

Prayer:

Dear God, thank you for leading me. For your direction and deliverance and for being with me. Please help me draw closer to you and never let me quit moving up your mountain. Please help me if I fall, get distracted, or am waylaid by the enemy. I thank you, knowing that I will be okay because your reign will last forever and ever, in Jesus' name, Amen.

None Like You, God

Scripture:

*Who is like you among the gods, O LORD—glorious
in holiness, awesome in splendour, performing
great wonders? You raised your right hand,
and the earth swallowed our enemies.*

~ Exodus 15:11-12 NLT

Woman of God:

Consider this scripture. How astounding is the display of the God we serve? They saw God's holiness and splendour and the mighty works of His hands. They were in awe by how God delivered them from their enemies. At this point, the Israelites could say, *who is like you, God?* On occasion, the daily activities of life can render you forgetful or give you selective memory, whereby you quickly forget the goodness of God, what he has done for you, or even who He is. Use these times as a marker to stir yourself up and become accustomed to giving thanks and praise to this incredible God no matter what is occurring in life. It honours Him. If your memory is cloudy, start by giving God thanks for someone else. Soon you will recall all that you have to be thankful for. Declare out loud—or through your journaling—

who God is to you. Is He the Alpha and the Omega? Or the faithful, everlasting God? Is He unchanging and mighty in battle? Either way, He seeks a relationship with His creation: *you*. Reflect on who God is to you this week, enabling you to say, "*there is no God like you.*"

Reflection Questions:

- Are you still in awe of who God is and the wonders He performs for you?

- Can you say—with your hand on your heart—that there is, "*none like you, God?*"

- Are you drawing closer to God by knowing and spending time with Him?

Prayer:

Dear God, thank you that there is no other God like you. No one can compare to you and no one can compete with you. Thank you for being the one true living God. Please help me to remember who you are, what you have done for me, and what you've brought me through. Please help me give you thanks and praise every day for no other reason than you are God, in Jesus' name, Amen.

Exalt the LORD Our God

Scripture:

Exalt the LORD our God!
Bow low before his feet, for he is holy!

~ Psalm 99:5 NLT

Woman of God:

Throughout this section you have seen some characteristics of the living God. Hopefully, these few examples will give you reasons to exalt God. Thanks to the Creator, God of the universe, and all creation. To the Holy God who encounters every individual uniquely by drawing them close, of which you are one. You know the name of God, making fellowship with Him easy and personal, to the sacrificial God, who loved you so much that He came and died on the cross for you. He would not leave or forsake you and sent another like himself—the Holy Spirit—to dwell in you. God is the source of love which is available to you. God is the one who is just and fair in all His ways. The one who is sovereign above all others and the all-knowing God. The God who is unchangeable. The one who is your shelter and refuge and loves with an unfailing love. The God who keeps His Covenant with you and does not go back on his word. The God who reigns forever and ever with no end. These are a mere fraction of who God is and what He does. Please take the time to discover this for yourself. The psalmist had it correct: *how can anyone look at God and not want to bow down low in the presence of His holiness and praise Him from the rooftops?* God deserves praise just for who He is. Take time each day this week to find something new or forgotten to praise and thank God for.

Reflection Questions:

- Are you able to exalt God when meeting others?

- How spirited is your exaltation towards God?

- Is exaltation and praise a lifestyle you live? Can it become one?

Prayer:

Dear God, thank you for placing your breath in me. I exalt you for who you are. Forgive me when I have forgotten to exalt you for all the wonderful things you have done for me, for answered prayer, unexpected blessings, for the love and protection of my family and friends, and for keeping my life and destiny. I exalt you, my God. You alone are worthy of my praise; be exalted in heaven and on the earth, in Jesus' name, Amen.

Pillar Two:

Spiritual Growth

True Fulfillment in the
Sacred Place With God,
Know Who You Are.

"To Become One With the Divine God."

Face It, You're Chosen

Scripture:

*But you are not like that, for you are a chosen
people. You are royal priests, a holy nation,
God's very own possession. As a result, you can
show others the goodness of God, for he called
you out of the darkness into his wonderful light.*

~ 1 Peter 2:9 NLT

Woman of God:

There are times when you can spend endless hours, years, and
energy chasing jobs, promotions, and new titles. Seeking
recognition, appreciation, or even validation can be influenced by many
factors. From the world or due to a lack of self-esteem. The world will
never be able to truly appreciate or validate you. Perhaps, like King
Solomon, you may eventually conclude that it is meaningless and all
is vanity. This scripture says you are a chosen people, royal priests, a
holy nation. You are chosen and predestined by God to perform some
specific task that only you can fulfill. Jesus is your High Priest and
King. Therefore, you and all believers are part of the royal priesthood.
Jesus fulfilled all conditions as the perfect slain lamb, once and for all.

Now you can enter the presence of God because of His sacrifice. The only sacrifice you need to bring is one of thanksgiving, praise, and a repentant heart. You are a holy nation because you are God's. You are His very own possession. When you realise this, there is no need to chase the world for titles; they would not be able to value you as God does. Spend time in the Word to know your true identity. When you truly know who you are, the influences of the world—for position and power—will fall away. You belong to God. You were purchased at a high cost. You're highly favoured and loved. Face it, you're chosen. This week, reflect on who you are in Christ Jesus and if you are aligned with what He says about you.

Reflection Questions:

- Do you struggle with worldly achievements and values?

- Do you know your identity in Christ Jesus?

- What are your thoughts on the titles Jesus has given you?

Prayer:

Dear God, thank you for your Word showing me who I am. Forgive me when I struggle with low self-esteem and forget what your Word says about me. Please help me believe and receive all you say about me above other voices, in Jesus' name, Amen.

Anointed of God

Scripture:

*The Spirit of the LORD is upon me, for he has anointed me
to bring Good News to the poor. He has sent me to proclaim
that captives will be released, that the blind will see,
that the oppressed will be set free, and that
the time of the LORD's favour has come.*

~ Luke 4:18-20 NLT

Woman of God:

In the Old Testament, anointing oil was used only by kings, priests, and prophets. You may recall the story of Samuel anointing the shepherd boy, David, to become God's chosen leader of Israel. Samuel used real oil and anointed David's head. The Old Testament oil represented the true living oil in the New Testament, the Holy Spirit of God. The scripture says Jesus was anointed for a specific task and accomplished all, from preaching the Good News, setting all kinds of captives free, healing the sick, and so much more. For a believer, the oil is the infilling of the Holy Spirit and His empowerment for ministry, of which you have been equipped with the necessary giftings to achieve the task. God has chosen and anointed you, set you apart as His own, to fulfill a specific purpose.

Jesus fulfilled the old prophet's prophecies in scripture and David became a king anointed of the prophet Samuel. Know that everything you need to succeed is already within you, regardless of whether you know what that is. Take heart because God knows there may be areas that need more sanctification or the holiness of Him. Nevertheless, God still has a special assignment for you as an anointed one of God, which you were born to fulfill and will complete. This week, reflect on what God has anointed you to complete.

Reflection Questions:

- What are your thoughts about being set apart for God's plan?

- What do you think the plan will entail?

- What are your thoughts about being equipped for a specific task?

Prayer:

Dear God, thank you for anointing me for a specific task regardless of whether I know what it is. I know I will complete it with you. Forgive me when I struggle. Please lead me by your Holy Spirit and guide me. I trust you and love you, in Jesus' name, Amen.

All Authority

Scripture:

> "Yes," he told them, "I saw Satan fall from heaven
> like lightening! Look, I have given you authority over
> all the power of the enemy, and you can walk among snakes
> and scorpions and crush them. Nothing will injure you."
>
> ~ Luke 10:18-19 NLT

Woman of God:

Have you ever wondered how nervous the disciples must have been to go out on their first-ever ministry assignment? Jesus informed them that the chief adversary fell from heaven and He gave them authority over all the enemy's power. Do you realise the extent of this power? Think about it this way. Most people work 9-5 jobs and hold positions that they enjoy in whichever field they specialise in. If you are fortunate, you will have a perfect boss or manager to ensure your well-being. However, this is not always the case, as you might be aware of. Maybe you have an overbearing manager who lords their power over your position and makes life intolerable for you. "*What's the point?*" you ask. Well, even though these bosses or managers have power over you, there is possibly another person they have to answer to. For instance, the owner of the company or the CEO, who has authority and all power. Jesus did not just give the disciples power over the enemy; he gave them authority and all power over the enemy. Therefore, no adversary, circumstance, or difficulty is over you or can compete with Jesus. His authority and all power are ultimate. Remember, Jesus said you can step on the enemy without harm. Know your position in Christ Jesus and fight from there. You are the head not the tail. This week, reflect on Jesus giving you authority and all power.

Reflection Questions:

- How have the power dynamics of others affected you? How did you cope?

- Do you walk in the authority and power Jesus gave you?

- Do you see yourself as Jesus sees you—as the head and not the tail?

Prayer:

Dear God, thank you for giving me authority and all power. Please guide me through your Holy Spirit to engage where I must. Forgive me if I have used any of your giftings in an unworthy manner. Please help me use all you have given me in a righteous and just way, in Jesus' name, Amen.

The Scriptures Say

Scripture:

But Jesus told him, "No! The Scriptures say, 'People do not live by bread alone, but by every word that comes from the mouth of God.'"
Then the devil took him to the holy city, Jerusalem, to the highest point of the Temple, and said, "If you are the Son of God, jump off! For the Scriptures say, 'He will order his angels to protect you. And they will hold you up with their hands so you won't even hurt your foot on a stone.'" Jesus responded, "The Scriptures also say, 'You must not test the LORD your God.'"

~ Matthew 4:4-7 NLT

Woman of God:

In the beginning, Eve succumbed to deception from a cunning adversary, with a trap using similar tactics by twisting words. Unfortunately, Eve let her eyes move her flesh with pride and, eventually, she and Adam fell from the grace of God as sin entered the world through disobedience. Humanity could have despaired at this point. Thankfully, your Redeemer Jesus came to undo the fall. This scripture shows that Jesus faced the worst temptation after a 40-day fast without food and water. Others would have yielded here through delirium and sheer exhaustion, but not Jesus. Even though He was weary, he did not let the adversary use God's words against him. He fought with them. This lesson Jesus teaches is to know the Word of God. When you feast upon it by eating and drinking the Word—like it is tangible food—you will say like Jesus, "*The Scripture says,*" or "*It is written.*" You cannot stand any other way. This is the only way to stand and fight against the adversary or any situation you are facing. It is not in your strength you battle but in God's, through His word. God fights for you. Learn to use the Word to stand on these promises: the Word is life, healing, victory, and transformation. The Word is God. This week, reflect on how you appropriate the Word of God in your life.

Reflection Questions:

- When the hardships—or the adversary come—how do you usually respond?

- What are your thoughts on the temptation of Jesus?

- What are your thoughts on using the Word to change your life?

Prayer:

Dear God, thank you for your Word and for showing me the correct way to fight. Forgive me when I don't appropriate your Word in my life or circumstance. Please help me to battle like Jesus did with the living Word, in Jesus' name, Amen.

Access to the King

Scripture:

Go and gather together all the Jews of Susa and fast for me.
Do not eat or drink for three days, night or day. My maids
and I will do the same. And then, though it is against the law,
I will go in to see the king. If I must die, I must die.'

~ Esther 4:16 NLT

Woman of God:

Esther was a young Jewish virgin woman plucked from obscurity in Susa. She was taken as a possible candidate for queen and then positioned in the palace. Do you think she ever envisioned this for her life? If you know the story, a plot was hatched to annihilate every Jew in the province, and beyond, by their enemy. Mordecai was Esther's uncle and he reminded her in Esther 4:14, *"Who knows if perhaps you were made queen for just such a time as this?"* Esther now had to contemplate doing the unthinkable. She knew going before the king, unsummoned, carried a punishment of death. She boldly declared, *"If I die, I die."* This outcome did not faze her. Esther knew who her God was. She had access to the King of kings so she rallied her people to fast and pray for three days. They needed to humble themselves and enter God's presence. Only God can turn the king's heart favourably towards Esther. Think about that. Are there any needs the King can help you with? You have direct access to the King of kings, 24/7. So bring your petitions, requests, heart desires, life issues, and struggles before Him. There is no matter too small and none too big that is impossible for the King of kings to address. He loves you. Bring them all. This week, reflect on Esther's boldness and courage and what you can learn from her story in your own life.

Reflection Questions:

- How do you feel about having direct access to the King?

- When in trouble, do you remember to go directly to the King?

- Are you aware of the benefits of praying and fasting as part of your lifestyle?

Prayer:

Dear God, thank you for giving me 24/7 access to your presence and being there when I need to talk to you. Forgive me when I forget to go to You first instead of last. Please help me to trust You as Esther did. Please help me to love being in Your presence, like my life depends on it, knowing my help comes from you, in Jesus' name, Amen.

The King Fights and Protects You

Scripture:

So Shadrach, Meshach, and Abednego, securely tied,
fell into the roaring flames. But suddenly Nebuchadnezzar
jumped up in amazement and exclaimed to his advisers,
"Didn't we tie up three men and throw them into the furnace?"
"Yes, Your Majesty, we certainly did," they replied. "Look!"
Nebuchadnezzar shouted. "I see four men, unbound, walking
around in the fire unharmed! And the fourth looks like a god!"

~ Daniel 3:23-25 NLT

Woman of God:

Being a follower of Jesus and a child of the living God means you will encounter troubles and difficulties through this association. The Word says that Jesus suffered persecution so you should expect the same as a follower. Take courage as you look at this scripture. These young Hebrew men defied the king to honour their God and practices. They refused to bow to the culture of the land and had faith that God would deliver them. But even if He did not save them, they still refused to obey the king's command. How encouraging is their faith and belief in God! You have a God who fights for you; the fourth person in the flaming fire. A 24/7 God who never sleeps nor slumbers. He fights for you so you can keep your peace. Even in dire situations, He will never abandon you or forsake you. He is Mighty and undefeated in battle. Above all things and situations, you are His child and He will defend you. So don't give up the faith. Arise and engage again. Know who and whose you are. God is with you. You have what it takes. Let your faith arise. You can do this; you are not alone. The King of kings fights to protect you. Have strong faith in him and watch your circumstances change. Reflect on where you need the King to fight on your behalf this week.

Reflection Questions:

- Do you trust God to be the fourth person in your fire?

- How protected do you feel knowing God never sleeps or slumbers?

- Do you have the confidence to battle, knowing God is with you?

Prayer:

Dear God, thank you for being a God who is undefeated and never sleeps or slumbers. Thank you for defending me and the people I love in my life. Forgive me when I have not wanted to engage in the battle so I would have a peaceful life. Please help me know that with you on my side, I cannot lose. I am an overcomer, in Jesus' name, Amen.

The Fear of the LORD

Scripture:

Fear of the LORD is the foundation of wisdom.
Knowledge of The Holy One results in good judgement.

~ Proverbs 9:10 NLT

Woman of God:

A fundamental aspect of standing well in your faith relates to knowing *The Fear of the LORD*. This does not refer to fear in the sense of being afraid of God, but more of a reverence and respect for God. Do you know the story of Ananias and Sapphira? The church gave birth to new followers who donated all they had for the ministry. However, Ananias and Sapphira, his wife, decided to sell their property and were untruthful to Peter and—more importantly—to the Holy Spirit. They conspired to hold back a portion of the sale, claiming they gave the whole amount, which showed a lack of fear of the LORD. They did not have reverence, respect or awe of God. They did not consider that God is all-knowing, holy, and mighty. In today's culture, some see God as their buddy or best mate, which can be extremely dangerous. Never lose sight of who God is. God is holy, righteous, powerful, sovereign, and can do as He wills. Through spiritual growth and discovery in your journey together, expect to personalize who God intimately is to you. Your Deliverer, Victor, and Miracle Worker. Ensure it is always with respect and reverence which comes from this relationship with God. Never lose sight of the fear of the LORD in reverence. Ananias and Sapphira's lack thereof cost them their lives. This week, reflect on your reverence and respect for God.

Reflection Questions:

- What do you think about the fear of the LORD?

- What are your thoughts on Ananias and Sapphira?

- Do you have a healthy reverence and respect for God?

Prayer:

Dear God, thank you for showing me what the fear of the LORD means. Please help me have reverence, awe, and respect for you and all your ways. Please help me not to forget who you are and forgive me when I do. Please draw me closer to you, daily, in Jesus' name, Amen.

Let Your Roots Grow Deep in the Word

Scripture:

But they delight in the law of the LORD, meditating on it day and night. They are like trees planted along the river-bank, bearing fruit each season. Their leaves never wither, and they prosper in all they do.

~ Psalm 1:2-3 NLT

Woman of God:

This is a picturesque image of how to stay strong in your walk with God. The psalmist here uses nature to convey a way of standing. Often, this can be difficult as the world bombards the flesh and soul with endless pleasures or meaningless scrolls of media feeds to engage with, which have no bearing on your life or future. It can be very easy to succumb to this out of comfort, loneliness, or to dull some pain. However, ceasing or changing habits is sometimes challenging when no strong anchor exists. Fortunately, with God, all things are possible, and the Psalmist tells you how to achieve this by meditating on scripture day and night. Not just occasionally or when you feel like it, but day and night. The delight grows when you keep pondering over the Word, taking in those promises and noticing this exceptional God. Picture the scenery of this tree planted by the river bank, bearing fruit in each season. It did not wither or die, and prosperity came. Now, picture you as that tree and spending time in God's presence as part of your lifestyle. You were intimately placed there by God, who is your life-giving source. Your roots will grow deep in the water of the Word, absorbing all the life-giving nutrients, causing you to bear much fruit and prosper due to the proper connection. This week, let your reflection focus on meditation of this scripture day and night.

Reflection Questions:

- When was the last time you delighted in God's word?

- What does mediation look like? Will it be part of your life moving forward?

- What do you think your roots look like? What can you do about it?

Prayer:

*Dear God, thank you for loving me and planting me
in the best resource for my life, in You. I thank you because
I know you want me to succeed and prosper. Forgive me
when I drift away from you or lose my attention. Please
help me to ponder day and night on Jesus the living
Word by your Holy Spirit, in Jesus' name, Amen.*

Let Your Faith Arise

Scripture:

While he was still speaking to her, messengers arrived from the home of Jairus, the leader of the synagogue. They told him, "Your daughter is dead. There's no use troubling the Teacher now." But Jesus overheard them and said to Jairus, "Don't be afraid. Just have faith."

~ Mark 5:35-36 NLT

Woman of God:

When surrounded by life's complications, it can challenge your faith, which may even lead you to question whether you had any. This is quite natural. Sometimes the unusual can shake you but do not remain there. In this story, when those messengers came with this word for Jairus, that could have been the end and the grieving process would have begun. Perhaps it is easier to give up rather than believe. When doubt creeps in, you question whether God heard your prayers. At the same time, you may be wondering whether the situation will ever change. But notice how Jesus quickly comforted Jairus with the words, *don't be afraid, have faith.* Maybe your faith needs this reassurance. God will not give you up or give more than you can bear. And yes, it may be painful and immensely frustrating, but whatever you face, keep going.

Where you are now is not your destination. Keep believing and let your faith arise. Persevere in your faith by trusting God to come through for you. Focus on Him. Do not allow your circumstances to dictate terms and conditions. Speak faith over yourself, your family, and situations. Jairus did not give in to that moment. He dared to have faith in Jesus—which was rewarded—and his daughter was saved. This week, reflect on the words of Jesus, *"Don't be afraid. Just have faith."*

Reflection Questions:

- What happens when your faith gets shaken?

- How do you reassure yourself to keep persevering in faith?

- What would an unshakable faith look like? What might you do to achieve this?

Prayer:

Dear God, thank you for reassuring my faith in this message.
Thank you for helping me to realign my faith back to
you and knowing that nothing is impossible for you.
Please do not let anything rob me of my faith
or belief in you, in Jesus' name, Amen.

Higher Thoughts

Scripture:

"My thoughts are nothing like your thoughts," says the LORD.
"And my ways are far beyond anything you could imagine.
For just as the heavens are higher than the earth,
so are my ways are higher than your ways
and my thoughts higher than your thoughts."

~ Isaiah 55:8-9 NLT

Woman of God:

This scripture states God's thoughts and ways are so different and higher than yours, which infers you need God to know God. Maybe this is why it cautions you not to lean on your understanding. Only by spending time in the Word and with the Word can you build a relationship with the Holy Spirit and honestly know God. Getting to know the Holy Spirit means investing in this relationship consciously. As far as relationships go, this is the most crucial of all relationships you will ever have for the promotion of your well-being and to discover the purpose of God. The Holy Spirit is not an it or a thing but a person. You must cultivate a relationship with the Holy Spirit to know God's thoughts. Only He can help you understand God's mind, heart, and thoughts because He is the Spirit of the living God. Talk with the Holy Spirit. It is imperative to connect with Him. He is the One who will reveal all truth to you and give insight into your queries. Ask Him your questions. Do not be surprised when He answers you. After all, you are His sheep. Build on this relationship until you can clearly distinguish between His voice and any other voice and until you know His thoughts and ways. This week, reflect on God's thoughts and ways and how different they are from your own.

Reflection Questions:

- What do you think about God's ways being beyond your imagination?

- How much time do you spend with the Holy Spirit to know Him?

- How meaningful is your relationship with the Holy Spirit?

Prayer:

Dear God, thank you for showing me that I need you to know you. Thank you for sending your Holy Spirit to be with me and reside within me. Forgive me for neglecting this relationship and not realizing its importance. Holy Spirit, please forgive me and help me talk to you and know you more intimately from now on, in Jesus' name, Amen.

Search Your Heart

Scripture:

Before each young woman was taken to the king's bed, she was given the prescribed twelve months of beauty treatment—six months with oil of myrrh, followed by six months with special perfumes and ointments.

~ Esther 2:12 NLT

Woman of God:

Are you aware that Esther had a year of spa treatments before meeting the king? She was blessed indeed! Granted, it's not possible for most women today—through busyness and the sheer number of varying activities—to lend to this pastime. And even if you were to marry a modern-day king, this would probably not be a requirement, more the pity. Esther enjoyed this treatment as requested by the king. However, are you able to make time to indulge in the same? It is essential to take time away from engagements and endless interactions. A place of solitude for self-reflection, a mental check-up, to be still, quiet, and pampered. Be free to take stock of what is happening in your life, whether you are on target or drifting. Do you need to change your eating habits or incorporate some new exercise for fitness? Are you an overthinker suffering from being overwhelmed, or a burden bearer? You have one life and one temple and must take care of both. Moreover, when things build up within you, it could impact your health if not dealt with. So, it would be best to make the time. It does not have to be a year. However, there are endless possibilities. Consider one day each month, a weekend away every month or quarter, a few hours sitting in silence, or simply take a walk in the park. This week, think about the last time you purposefully took time off—or time away—for yourself.

Reflection Questions:

- When did you last take yourself away for a pampering spa or an outing with friends?

- Do you think it's vital to take self-checks regarding your health?

- Do you find it easy to take a break? Can you change this?

Prayer:

Dear God, thank you for helping me understand it is okay to take time away for myself, whether in the spa or other activities. Forgive me when I do not prioritise myself. Please help me understand I cannot do all things by myself. I have one body and one life. Please help me to become whole and healthy for my journey, in Jesus' name, Amen.

Draw Closer to Me

Scripture:

*When you pray, don't be like the hypocrites who love to
pray publicly on street corners and in the synagogues where
everyone can see them. I tell you the truth, that is all the reward
they will ever get. But when you pray, go away by yourself,
shut the door behind you, and pray to your Father in private.
Then your Father, who sees everything, will reward you.*

~ Matthew 6:5-6 NLT

Woman of God:

Often, a believer's prayer life can be challenging to nonexistent. The more you want to pray, the further away you appear. You may not be alone here. If this is you, at least you know your prayer life. The hypocrites in this scripture were possibly unaware. Their prayers were for the pomp and glory of their status for the crowds. Looking at the scripture shows how God sees the act of prayer as intimate. He tells you to go to a room privately and close the door behind you. It could pose a challenge if you are in the park or outdoors, so the door could mean distractions and remaining focused. Prayer happens behind the scenes between a Father and daughter, and it's an intimate discussion in a sacred space where you can share your heart's most profound expression. Everything you share is confidential and will not be divulged to the neighbourhood. Talk and present all your needs before a loving Father. Only He can grant your request or provide a new strategy to overcome your issues. Above all, try to keep the communication lines open. Remember, the more you pray, the more you draw closer to God whilst learning to battle. The more you learn to battle, the stronger your faith will become because you know who has your back. So, pray without ceasing to grow spiritually then watch your life turn around. This week, reflect on how prayer is an intimate space between you and the Father.

Reflection Questions:

- Have you ever struggled with prayer? How did you change it?

- Do you feel intimately connected to Father God whilst praying?

- Can you maintain your focus without becoming distracted?

Prayer:

Dear God, thank you for being attentive to me and answering my prayers in your time and your way. Forgive me when I struggle, and prayer feels like a chore. Please help me see that prayer is my communication line for life, in Jesus' name, Amen.

Pillar Three:

Personal Growth

Encouragement for
Self-Development, Persevere
Through the Journey.

"Fortitude for Your Race."

Seek Him with All Your Heart

Scripture:

If you look for me wholeheartedly, you will find me.

~ Jeremiah 29:13 NLT

Woman of God:

Can you recall when someone first caught your attention? Whether from primary school, at work, or a social event? That day when your neck turned, your heart skipped a beat, your knees buckled, and your imagination started to run wild. You know what I mean! You wanted to be around this person constantly, make conversation, see if they noticed you, and be wherever they were. Like being drawn by a magnet. Now think back to the moment Jesus captured your attention. A spiritual, supernatural event occurred in your heart and, in an instant, your whole world changed. Do you remember what this felt like when your world now revolved only around Him? You are eager to spend every waking breath with Him, to be in His presence, as if there were not enough hours in the day. You were searching wholeheartedly to find Him by learning of Him and telling everyone about Him, and

He became unique and significant to you. Hold tight to this recollection. Nurture this relationship far above any other interaction you will have. Sometimes, you can forget who Jesus is and how important He is to you. He gave everything for you, the one He loves. Let Him become your everything again. Search for Him afresh with your whole heart. You will find Him. This week, reflect on that time. Seek Him once more, and remain in that moment.

Reflection Questions:

- How did God capture your attention on your first encounter? How was it memorable for you?

- Do you still seek after God with all your heart?

- Have you wandered from the place of awe and excitement in your relationship with God? What might you do to recover it?

Prayer:

*Dear God, thank you for first loving me and accepting me.
Thank you for the moment you caught my attention.
Forgive me when I have forgotten or have become cold
or indifferent. Forgive me for being consumed
with worldly distractions of life. Please re-kindle that
flame of passion for my first love within my heart,
to always remain close to you, and to enjoy new levels
of intimacy with you, in Jesus' name, Amen.*

God Knows You

Scripture:

You saw me before I was born. Every day of my life
was recorded in your book. Every moment was
laid out before a single day had passed.

~ Psalm 139:16 NLT

Woman of God:

This scripture is quite mind-blowing. It says the God of the universe knows you. He knew you before yesterday, today, and tomorrow. God saw you before you were born and knows your every moment. No one on this earth can ever say that about you. Do you ever feel that no matter how much you share with other people, they don't get you? People may feel like they know who you are, but they do not truly know you. People know about you with what you share with them. They cannot claim they know what makes you... you! Only God knows you fully and wholly in your innermost being. Reflect on that. God created you to walk, live, and have fellowship with Him. This earth would not be complete without you. God knows precisely what you are like, how you think and feel, and what makes you happy or angry. You are not a revelation to the God who created you, so do not condemn yourself when you get things wrong. He knows all these things about you and you are still precious to Him. Keep hold of the God who created all things. This week, try reflecting on this: God knows you intimately, created you by design, and you have a right to be here on this earth.

Reflection Questions:

- When reflecting on how God recorded your life in His book, what springs to mind?

- Do you struggle to believe how much God knows you?

- What has God revealed to you through this message?

Prayer:

Dear God, thank you for reminding me today that you know me. Please help me surrender and let you into any areas of doubt and difficulties I face. Forgive me when I forget that you are the God who knew me before I was born and that you know what is best for me. Forgive me when I forget that you first created me for a relationship with you. Thank you for making me feel known today, in Jesus' name, Amen.

The God Who Sees You

Scripture:

Thereafter, Hagar used another name to refer to the LORD,
who had spoken to her. She said, "You are the God who sees me."
She also said, "Have I truly seen the One who sees me?"

~ Genesis 16:13 NLT

Woman of God:

Have you ever felt like you cannot see a way through your trials in life? So much so that you want to run away from your problems? Last week highlighted the God who knows you, and this week calls attention to the God who sees you. Do you know the story of Hagar? It is quite a sad one. She was an enslaved Egyptian servant and a handmaid to Sarai. Sarai mistreated Hagar to fulfill God's promise of an heir, and her husband Abram satisfied his wife's demands. Hagar became pregnant, and the relationship went downhill, so Hagar ran off. She met an angel of God near a spring of water, which changed her life as she poured out her grievances. The angel told her about her future child and descendants. More importantly, he told her that God heard her cry of distress. She did not encounter at that moment God as Yahweh—LORD. Hagar met with El Roi, the God who sees me.

How amazing is this? God saw her right where she was. You may be in a similar space right now, wondering if God sees you and what you are going through. Remember, God knows and sees you. He is with you. This week, reflect on your heartaches and deep longings, like Hagar, and pour them out before El Roi.

Reflection Questions:

- Do you know God as El Roi, the God who sees you?

- Do you find it easy or difficult to open your heart to God?

- Can you remember the last time God met you somewhere unexpected? What happened?

Prayer:

Dear God, thank you for being El Roi, the God who sees me when I cannot see a way through my dilemma. Please help me trust and believe you see the bigger picture of my life. Forgive me when I want to run far away from you and my pain. Forgive me when I want to handle obstacles in my strength, out of control, or out of necessity. Please help me not to run away from you but towards you. I trust you because you see me, in Jesus' name, Amen.

Seasons of Life

Scripture:

For everything there is a season,
a time for every activity under heaven.

~ Ecclesiastes 3:1 NLT

Woman of God:

You might be in a difficult position right now. Feeling like the Israelites—who spent 40 years on an eleven-day journey—wondering when this season will end. If you have ever felt like this, chances are you're not alone. You may have imagined yourself somewhere else, doing something else, with someone else, and the list goes on and on. Sometimes, the seasons seem lengthy and bleak, and you may want to cry, "Why me?" It can be frustrating, as doubt wants to creep in to make you question where God is and what He is doing. Here, you need to learn to appreciate the seasons. As harsh as that sounds, hold on. God knows. Each season brings different kinds of lessons, conditions, and challenges. How you cope in one season may require new skills in the next. Woman of God, hang in there! Fortunately, seasons are always in a state of change. They always produce something, even when you cannot tell what that is. But each season has a part to play in your life, bringing comfort, discomfort, pain, or joy. As the scripture says, there is a season for everything. A time for everything under heaven. Your season may seem hidden, demanding, or unsure. Be assured it is not that way for God. Trust God through the season. He will be with you when you come out on the other side and He will receive the glory. Remind yourself the season will change and a new season will soon begin. Reflect on whatever season you are in this week, and praise God for it anyway.

Reflection Questions:

- Does this season feel like a repetitive cycle or is it joyous?

- Can you recognise what you have learned or what God did during this season?

- How have you managed unexpected seasons in life?

Prayer:

Dear God, thank you for being with me every season and bringing me through it. Please help me when I struggle in the unknown season, whether good or challenging. Please forgive me when I moan or grumble in the discomfort of uncertainty or lack of trust in you. Please help me to know you will work it out for my good. Thank you for the season lessons you have taught me, in Jesus' name, Amen.

Favour of the King

Scripture:

When he saw Queen Esther standing there in the inner court,
he welcomed her and held out the gold sceptre to her.
So Esther approached and touched the end of the sceptre.
Then the king asked her, "What do you want, Queen Esther?
What is your request? I will give it to you,
even if it is half the kingdom!"

~ Esther 5:2-3 NLT

Woman of God:

In the spiritual growth section, you read about Esther's boldness. A brief recap: to go unsummoned before the king carried serious repercussions. It meant your funeral plan had to be paid for and put in place. Esther knew this, but still she went. Imagine this long walk towards the king filled with trepidation and tinged with apprehension. Nevertheless, in faith, she stepped out and moved. As she approached the king, something astonishing happened. The king was delighted to see her and held out the gold sceptre. Before Esther opened her mouth, he publicly announced that he would grant her request, even by giving her half the kingdom. God is so awe-inspiring! God sent this favour and blessing ahead of Esther. She did not even say a word. She positioned herself before the king, and the favour of God met her there. Just know one thing today: the King of kings is holding out His gold sceptre to you, enquiring, *"Woman of God, what can I do for you, and what do you want?"* Do not let fear or life's many circumstances keep you from the presence of the King. He has incredible blessings and favour just for you. If you are scared, that is perfectly fine. Go anyway! Do not allow hindrances to keep you from blessings that may change your life instantly. Only the King can do this. This week, reflect on positioning yourself in the presence of the King of kings.

Reflection Questions:

- Think about the King's sceptre pointed towards you. What is your request?

- Have you stepped out in faith even when you felt scared? What happened?

- Can you recall the unexpected blessings given by the King without you asking?

Prayer:

Dear God, thank you for the good gifts of heaven which only come from you. Thank you for your favour and blessing over my life. Forgive me when I forget to thank you for the miraculous things you do in my life. Please help me remember that you reward those who seek you, in Jesus' name, Amen.

Be Strong and Courageous

Scripture:

This is my command—be strong and courageous!
Do not be afraid or discouraged. For the LORD
your God is with you wherever you go.

~ Joshua 1:9 NLT

Woman of God:

Do you know that before Saul became king, he was so afraid he ran away and hid? Maybe this is a typical response when faced with unexpected changes, the unknown, or new opportunities in life. However, faith dictates to not allow the circumstance to lead you. Joshua may have had many doubts: *How do I follow a great leader like Moses?* God did not allow those doubts to take root. He commanded Joshua to be strong, courageous, and unafraid because He would be with him. God met Joshua in a place that could have had him running in the opposite direction. You may be facing something similar. It may be holding your spirit captive with the outcome of making you shrink back and not venturing forward. But keep persisting. God said He would be with you wherever you go. Be encouraged today. You do not travel alone, even if the terrain of life is presenting something new or downright scary. God is commanding you to be strong and courageous. You may not slay all your dragons in one day but start somewhere. Do not worry if you feel you have no strength or courage. God has it in abundance and will readily give it to you freely. Just ask Him. Declare to that new or scary territory today that God is with you. Reflect on being strong and courageous and God being with you wherever you go this week.

Reflection Questions:

- When greeted with a new challenge or the unexpected, what is your usual response?

- How do you feel knowing God is with you wherever you are?

- Is anything in your life making you shrink from God's best for you?

Prayer:

Dear God, thank you for the promise you will be with me wherever I go. Thank you for encouraging me to be strong and courageous. Forgive me when I am slow to act out of fear. Please help me press in and move forward with my purpose. Please let this land in my spirit: that I can do everything because you are with me, in Jesus' name, Amen.

Fear Not

Scripture:

Don't be afraid, for I am with you. Don't be discouraged for I am your God. I will strengthen you and help you. I will hold you up with my victorious right hand.

~ Isaiah 41:10 NLT

Woman of God:

How much energy do you spend being afraid, fearful, or worrying about varying aspects of life? God created you and knows your nature. He ensured that He would tell you often through the Scriptures not to fret, worry, or be in fear. When you're afraid, it leads to discouragement and it robs you of obtaining what you need. Think about this: if God told you He is with you and not to be afraid, and there is nothing more prominent or more significant than God. Maybe it is time to be honest with yourself. Do you believe Him? God does not want you to be in fear because it hampers your faith. It also hampers your connection with God because you are preoccupied with what you fear. The scripture says that perfect love casts out all fear, and you know the source of love is God. Therefore, be encouraged because you can seek God at any time to help you. He will show you what this fear is rooted in. When you discover this together, God's strength will uproot it and pull it up and out. Rise in your faith and heed the scripture above. Let God give you strength. He said not to fear. He will uphold you with his victorious right hand and none can take you from it. Reflections for this week: look at your life and see if there are any areas where you might be afraid and need God's love and His hand.

Reflection Questions:

- Do you overly worry or have a fearful nature? What is that like for you?

- The last time you worried or were fearful, what did it rob you of in your life?

- Can you trust God's loving hands to come through for you?

Prayer:

Dear God, thank you for telling me not to fear.
Please forgive me when I do. Please remove everything
that is not of you in my life. From doubt and confusion
to frustration and unbelief. Please uproot it all and bring
me freedom. Please help me to live victoriously in
every area of my life, in Jesus' name, Amen.

Confidence in God

Scripture:

And I am certain that God, who began the good work within you, will continue his work until it is finally finished on the day when Christ Jesus returns.

~ Philippians 1:6 NLT

Woman of God:

Occasionally, many hours can be spent on negative mindsets or belief systems that do not want to change. Then, you might blame yourself and become your harshest critic, making you feel terrible for not accomplishing a task or changing a habit. Sometimes, you can be so busy trying to change and perfect yourself that you forget that God created you. You may also have to accept that there are some things you cannot do by yourself. You need God. But do not misunderstand. It is always good to develop and improve yourself, update new skills, and learn to be the best version of yourself. This scripture says the good work that God began within you, He will complete and finish on the day when Christ returns. Essentially, it is God's work. And this is where you can have confidence in God because what He started, He will finish. God's goal is to perfect you; changing you from glory to glory in the likeness of His Son Jesus. The next time that harsh critic comes around, calmly respond that God will do it. Let God change and rearrange anything that needs removal. This week, reflect upon the work God is doing within you while reminding yourself that it will be complete when Jesus Christ returns.

Reflection Questions:

- How does it make you feel, knowing that God will complete the work He has begun in you?

- What conversation might you have with your harsh critic now?

- Do you have the same or more confidence in God?

Prayer:

Dear God, thank you for the work you have begun within me. I know you will complete it. Forgive me when I struggle to do everything alone and do not call on you to help me. Please help me focus on your voice, not the critics or other voices, only on yours and the good things you want for me, in Jesus' name, Amen.

Keep Going

Scripture:

For I can do everything through Christ,
who gives me strength.

~ Philippians 4:13 NLT

Woman of God:

Running your race in life can often pose many challenges. Sometimes, you might not know the race, let alone where the racetracks are. Sometimes, you may want to give up when you do not see immediate rewards, validation, or appreciation for your efforts. You may question whether this is even the race you are supposed to run. You may even feel a little jealous. Others may seem off and running steadily with real stamina and endurance. You may feel like you are way behind and missed the starting shot. Regardless of what you think or what it looks like, do not compare yourself to to others. Focus on your race. Carry on. God has promised that you can do everything through Christ who strengthens you. Even if you feel discontent with what you are doing in life, keep going. New opportunities will come. Even if your business only has a few customers, keep going. You never know who will walk through your door next. And even if you do not know what to do, keep going. You will discover what it is in time, through your journey with Christ. He is the one who strengthens you and gives you the ability to do everything. As the Word says, apart from God, you can do nothing. With God, you have no limits. Wow! This week, reflect on completing your race through Christ who strengthens you.

Reflection Questions:

- Do you believe you can do all things through Christ who strengthens you?

- Do you have a mental picture of your race?

- How does running your race make you feel?

Prayer:

Dear God, thank you for your strength. Forgive me when I have become preoccupied and even jealous of other people's races and being ahead of me. I believe and trust that you will do everything you have said. Please help me discover the race you have for me and please help me run it well—with all my heart—for your glory, in Jesus' name, Amen.

Grateful Heart

Scripture:

> When the LORD brought back his exiles to Jerusalem,
> it was like a dream! We were filled with laughter, and
> we sang for joy. And the other nations said, "What amazing
> things the LORD has done for them." Yes, the LORD
> has done amazing things for us! What Joy!
>
> ~ Psalm 126:1-3 NLT

Woman of God:

Throughout the Old Testament, you can read how the Israelites struggled with who God was or even the wonders He had performed. This neglect can happen when busy or preoccupied with other life activities. But despite those lapses, the Old Testament also recalls when the exiles got it right. The scripture shows a time when they were in awe of God. When their deliverance felt like a dream. The Israelites were filled with laughter and sang for Joy, singing about what the LORD had done for them. Neighbouring communities seemed to agree with them of the goodness of God, as though it were tangible. Nonetheless, the enemy is cunning. He wants your hardship and issues to become your focal point. This enemy wants to keep you trapped in regret or distress whilst fabricating lies in your soul about the God you serve. At these times, you need to dust off the cobwebs and remember the goodness of God towards you. Learn to look back and remember what God has done for you and what He has brought you through. Let that put a smile back on your face, warm your heart, and put a skip in your step. Do not let the enemy steal your song or joy. Do not allow the busyness of life make you forgetful. God will remind you that He works all things out for your good. Reflect on everything God has done for you this week until that memory feels tangible.

Reflection Questions:

- Do you have a song expressing the amazing things God has done for you?

- Do you have times when you forget? What do you do to remember?

- When God blessed or delivered you, were you able to celebrate?

Prayer:

Dear God, thank you for the countless times you have come through for me and delivered me. Forgive me when I have forgotten to thank you in the moment or forgotten entirely. I take this opportunity to thank you for everything you have done for me; for all your goodness, mercy, and grace every day in my life, in Jesus' name, Amen.

Where is Your Trust

Scripture:

But those who trust in the LORD will find new strength.
They will soar high on wings like eagles. They will run
and not grow weary. They will walk and not faint.

~ Isaiah 40:31 NLT

Woman of God:

When the world revolves around you at lightning speed, it can be very easy to trust many things. Your job, monthly pay cheque, or your aspirations to become accomplished in a particular field. Things like your dreams, desire to be married, or a thriving business and meaningful relationships. Goals and visions are reasonable and give you direction to journey forward. The danger can arise when you solely put your trust in these things. However, God will lead you on which path to walk on. Maybe you have become discouraged when you trusted to aspire up the ladder or became estranged from your loved ones. Possibly, you trusted to be married already and no one has manifested for you in the natural. And the list goes on. This scripture tells you exactly where to place your trust. It says those who trust in the LORD will find new strength. Maybe you need the strength to wait, the strength to endure adversity, or the strength to still believe and go on. Equally exciting, the scripture goes on to say you will soar. The great thing about soaring is it provides a new perspective from a new position. Also, it says you will run and not grow weary; walk and not faint. You are covered. God wants you to trust Him so He can sustain and hold you. No matter your circumstances. This week, look and reflect on where you have placed your trust.

Reflection Questions:

- Can you recall what your trust was like when it was misplaced?

- Do you solely trust in God? If not, what might you do to change this?

- How do you feel knowing God will give you resources when you trust Him?

Prayer:

Dear God, thank you that I can place my trust in you, knowing you only want the best for me. Forgive me when I have placed my trust in other things and was upset and frustrated when things did not turn out as I expected. Forgive me when I even blamed you. Please help me to trust in you first and wholeheartedly, knowing that no one will ever love me like you do, in Jesus' name, Amen.

Following Jesus

Scripture:

And now, just as you accepted Christ Jesus as your Lord,
you must continue to follow him.

~ Colossians 2:6 NLT

Woman of God:

There is a story in the Bible where Jesus explained He was the true bread of life that came down from heaven. He spoke about His broken body as bread and His blood as wine, saying to the crowd they would need to eat and drink of Him to live. As you can imagine, this was not well received. Many followers did not understand and ceased to continue. Do you remember the time you first chose to follow Jesus? Did you discover it was not always easy? Did the way seem narrow? Did it come with a significant cost to you? This is where you need to be resolute. You believed in Jesus as the Saviour, who came to take away the world's sins by his death on the cross. Jesus fulfilled the will of Father God to pay your ransom out of love. This scripture says you must continue to follow Him. Jesus also said this in Matthew 9:9, *"Follow me and be my disciple."* When the way seems troublesome, remind yourself that you accepted Jesus' invitation. Be adamant not to let anything deter or sway you from this course. Those who turn back or do not continue will miss out on the most incredible relationship they could ever have. Remember that as you follow consistently after Jesus, your life becomes a testimony. It will encourage and lead others to do the same. This week, reflect upon the commitment you made to follow Jesus.

Reflection Questions:

- What was it like for you when you began to follow Jesus?

- Do you have any areas in your life where you need to renew your commitment?

- What has following Jesus cost you? What has following Him gained you?

Prayer:

Dear God, thank you for choosing me to follow Jesus.
Thank you, Jesus, for dying and giving your all for me.
Thank you for keeping me. Forgive me when I wander
away to follow after other things. Please help me remain
committed and strong enough to follow you because
I chose you and love you, in Jesus' name, Amen.

Pillar Four:

Purpose

Discover and Fulfill
your God-Given Purpose,
Utilize Giftings Within.

"The Architect's Master Plan."

Seek God for the Plan

Scripture:

"For I know the plans I have for you," says the LORD.
"They are plans for good and not for disaster,
to give you a future and a hope."

~ Jeremiah 29:11 NLT

Woman of God:

God says He has a plan for you. Perhaps you are blessed with this discovery or perhaps you spend countless hours trying to figure this out. Either way, it will be exclusive to you. Only you can fulfill and accomplish this work. In the next few weeks, you will see other stories from the Bible of how they navigated their plan. Sometimes, certain conditions are needed to bring you into alignment, which you will see through these life stories. Moreover, the fantastic thing about God's plan is that He knows it! So if you are unsure what it is for you, it's ok. This is a good place to start. Work on your relationship with God and get to know Him intimately. Then, as God speaks with you, you will discern His truth and see His plan for your life. God's plan will not harm you in any way. It's the only plan that guarantees a future and hope. You can rest assured that it is excellent for your life and the lives you will touch and interact with. God never creates anything without a purpose. Your participation is to seek it out. Find comfort that you are on God's mind; that He has thought about you. This week, reflect on God knowing you and having a plan specifically for you to fulfill.

Reflection Questions:

- How often have you thought about God's plan for your life?

- Do you trust and believe that God has a good plan for you?

- Are you ready to discover and embrace God's plan for your life?

Prayer:

Dear God, thank you for creating a unique plan,
especially for me. Thank you for saying that your plan will
not harm me and is for my good. Forgive me when I have
other ideas for my life or for not seeking your plan.
Please help me fulfill and accomplish the plan
you have for my life, in Jesus' name, Amen.

Rahab Believed in the Plan

Scripture:

Meanwhile, Joshua said to the two spies, "Keep your promise.
Go to the prostitute's house and bring her out, along with all her family."
The men who had been spies went in and brought out Rahab, her father,
mother, brothers, and all the other relatives who were with her. They
moved her whole family to a safe place near the camp of Israel.

~ Joshua 6:22-23 NLT

Woman of God:

In the story of Rahab, we learn that she lived as a prostitute in Jericho. The king sent a message to her concerning the two Israelite spies who entered the city. Evidently, she was well known. Rahab explained to the spies that they had heard of the wonders God performed for His people. The fame of their God terrified the inhabitants of Jericho. As the city cowered in fear, Rahab's faith rose. She dared to believe in the God who saved His people. Rahab kept the spies alive, knowing God would give them the city when they returned. God's plan for Rahab began the moment she believed in Him. Rahab had one request to the spies: the salvation of her household. The story unfolds with the city conquered. Rahab places a scarlet rope on her home and she and her entire family are delivered from destruction and death. Through this one act of faith, salvation came to her household. They walked out to freedom. Rahab went on to marry a prominent figure in Israel and became part of the lineage of Jesus. Regardless of her previous status, God fulfilled His plan in her life. She had a key and pivotal role to play in the strategic success of Israel. Rahab was precisely in the right place at the right time with the correct mindset. Remember, God has an incredible plan for you to fulfill. This week, reflect on whether His plan requires belief, faith, or something else from you.

Reflection Questions:

- Does your own belief or mindset need an overhaul for the plan?

- Does this story encourage you to find your God-given plan?

Prayer:

Dear God, thank you for your plan. I believe I will be in the right place at the right time to fulfill your purpose. Please remove any hindrances within me that will keep me from believing and trusting in you. Please help me step out into the fullness of what you have planned for my life, in Jesus' name, Amen.

Hannah's Need Touched God's Need for the Plan

Scripture:

Hannah was in deep anguish, crying bitterly as she prayed to the LORD. And she made this vow: "O LORD of Heaven's Armies, if you will look upon my sorrow and answer my prayer and give me a son, then I will give him back to you. He will be yours for his entire lifetime, and as a sign that he has been dedicated to the LORD, his hair will never be cut."

~ 1 Samuel 1:10-11 NLT

Woman of God:

Do you know the story of Hannah? She was a profoundly distressed woman. Even though she was married, her husband's other wife, Peninnah, would tease her because she was barren. Hannah could have stopped there and silently let her woe and despair defeat her. Her husband wanted to fill that space of deep longing, yet the desire for a child was too great. One day, in the presence of God, she cried silently for a child, speaking without words. Hannah vowed to present this child back to God for His service. Could you be this brave? Arguably, it would be fair to say that Hannah birthed a mighty prophet of God for Israel named Samuel. He was taken to Eli at a young age to join the priesthood. Moreover, Hannah fulfilled God's purposeful plan the moment her desire met God's plan for her life. Hannah's life changed from despair to a song of praise to God. Hannah needed a child, and God needed a righteous prophet. He also granted Hannah other children. Can your need touch God's plan? Perhaps it could mean using your existing gifts and talents or undiscovered ones. Or something entirely new. Maybe you will physically give birth like Hannah or maybe something utterly different—from thought to concept. Either way, you will be amazed at what God can do. This week, reflect on whether you have any deep yearnings you want God to grant you.

Reflection Questions:

- Can you give your desires to God and see what He will do?

- Do you feel you have something ready to birth? Have you talked with God about it?

- Are you accustomed to crying out to God for your needs?

Prayer:

Dear God, thank you for hearing my prayers and petitions when I present them to you. Forgive me when I cry alone without sharing my pains with you. Please continue to hold me in those moments with your love and grace, in Jesus' name, Amen.

Leah's Heart of Praise
for the Plan

Scripture:

*Once again Leah became pregnant and gave birth
to another son. She named him Judah,
for she said, "Now I will praise the LORD!"
And then she stopped having children.*

~ Genesis 29:35 NLT

Woman of God:

Do you know the story of Leah, the unloved woman? Jacob went to his mother's family and fell in love with the beautiful Rachel, whom he wanted to marry. He only had eyes for her. Unfortunately, she had a ruthless father who plotted against Jacob and swapped out one bride for another on the wedding day. Hence, Leah's predicament is that her husband does not love her. Her father said it was not their practice to marry off the younger daughter before the elder daughter. They might have mentioned that to Jacob. Yet, every time Leah gave birth, she said in her heart, *"Surely Jacob will love me now or show me some affection."* Alas, for poor downhearted Leah, it was not to be. Leah had given birth to three children, hoping to secure her husband's love. Finally, Leah had her fourth child and called him Judah, which means praise. She said, "*Now I will praise the LORD.*" It was difficult for Leah to see that she was walking in God's plan because she desperately yearned to be loved. She finally turned her attention to God. He was the one who blessed her with the fruit of the womb, who gave her children to love, and who would love her. Leah was part of God's purposeful plan. A tribe of nations came from her womb and despite her husband not loving her, she became thankful and praised God anyway. This week, reflect on something different each day to give God a heartfelt shout of praise.

Reflection Questions:

- What parts of Leah's story resonate with you?

- Can you praise God through your difficult moments? What's that like?

- Will you still trust God with the plan even if it's not what you expect?

Prayer:

Dear God, thank you that you have a plan for me and that you will work it out for my good. Forgive me when I struggle to understand what you are doing or when it does not look like how I imagined. Please give me the grace to accept and receive your gifts for me and to remain content and blessed because you are a good God, in Jesus' name, Amen.

Mary's Agreement for the Plan

Scripture:

Mary asked the angel, "But how can this happen? I am a virgin."
The angel replied, "The Holy Spirit will come upon you,
and the power of the Most High will overshadow you.
So the baby to be born will be holy, and he will be called the
Son of God. What's more, your relative Elizabeth has become
pregnant in her old age! People used to say she was barren,
but she has conceived a son and is now in her sixth month.
For the word of God will never fail." Mary responded,
"I am the LORD's servant. May everything you have said
about me come true." And then the angel left her.

~ Luke 1:34-38 NLT

Woman of God:

Think about this: Mary had a miraculous assignment. She had just become betrothed to Joseph, the pinnacle of a young girl's life. Out of nowhere, an angel of God appears with the strangest of news. Telling Mary she would become pregnant when the power of the Most

High overshadows her. The child she would bear is the Messiah, the world's Saviour. Mary responded with breathtaking faith for one so young. She said she was the LORD's servant. She was in agreement with everything he said would happen. Mary accepted God's plan. She agreed with what God wanted to accomplish through her. Mary did not ask for a moment to call a friend or discuss the plan with her family. She may have asked a question but there was no hesitation. She said yes to the plan. Sometimes, your plan supersedes God's plan, making it difficult to fulfill or come to pass. Mary overcame this as she exhibited a servant's heart. She only wanted to please and do the will of God. This week, reflect on whether you can accept God's plan for your life, no matter what it is. And whether you can give God your yes.

Reflection Questions:

- Can you say, *"God, let it be as you will for my life?"*

- What do you think about having a servant's heart like Mary?

- If God gave you an unusual assignment, how quickly would you accept it?

Prayer:

Dear God, thank you for being the author and finisher of my faith. Thank you for every word and promise spoken over me that will come to pass. Please help me have a servant's heart—like Mary's—and accept your perfect will for my life, in Jesus' name, Amen.

Naomi and Ruth's Alignment for the Plan

Scripture:

But Ruth replied, "Don't ask me to leave you and turn back. Wherever you go, I will go; wherever you live, I will live. Your people will be my people, and your God will be my God. Wherever you die, I will die, and there I will be buried. May the LORD punish me severely if I allow anything but death to separate us!" When Naomi saw that Ruth was determined to go with her, she said nothing more.

~ Ruth 1:16-18 NLT

Woman of God:

Every journey starts by taking a step and every journey needs the companionship of another. Perhaps this is your husband, best friend, family member, or other person who is not yet known. In the book of Ruth, we see Naomi's story unfold. She sets off on a journey with her family to escape the famine in Israel. Unfortunately, her prospects worsen in Moab. She and her daughters-in-law mourned the death of her husband and two sons. Naomi persuaded Orpah to return to her home. However, Ruth cleaved to her mother-in-law. Ruth set off with Naomi to a strange land, people, God, and customs. Arriving in Israel, Ruth captured Boaz's eyes and heart whilst gleaning in his field. As the closest relative, Boaz decided to redeem everything belonging to Naomi, including Ruth. A few challenges arose, but eventually they were married and had a child. Their child was named Obed. Obed fathered Jesse and Jesse fathered David, the future king of Israel. God orchestrated this alignment which brought such blessings to Naomi, Ruth, and Israel. You may need to discover if your God-given plan requires you to be in divine alignment with others, for its fulfillment. So be encouraged. God will equip you to fulfill His plan. This week, reflect on the relationship alignments God has already blessed you with and give thanks for them.

Reflection Questions:

- What do you think about Naomi's and Ruth's relationship?

- How are your relationships in comparison? Can they be improved?

- Do you hope for God to orchestrate something beautiful in your life?

Prayer:

*Dear God, thank you for your love and kindness
and the many good relationships you have given me.
Forgive me when I have mistreated them or taken them
for granted. Please help me to do better and to honour
every single one, in Jesus' name, Amen.*

Jesus Fulfilled the Plan of the Father

Scripture:

"But why did you need to search?" he asked.
"Didn't you know I must be in my Father's house?"

~ Luke 2:49 NLT

Woman of God:

After Jesus and his family spent a festive time of celebration in Jerusalem, they set off to go home. Mary and Joseph frantically searched the caravans, asking their relatives if they had seen their child. Jesus was missing. They immediately turned around and eventually found Jesus sitting with the religious teachers in the temple. Are you surprised Jesus stayed behind? At such a young age—just 12 years old—this must have been thrilling for Jesus. These religious scholars were astounded by His wisdom and knowledge, which seemed beyond His age. Jesus sat with them, listened, asked, and answered questions. Jesus was connecting with God's designed plan for His life and it was flowing through Him. Jesus was still feasting, eating, and drinking on the expounded Word of God. That must have been a joyous moment only to have two anxious parents tearing Him away. They were looking for their child not the Son of God. Jesus' asked why did they search for him? Did they not know He would be in His Father's house? Some versions of the Bible say *"His Father's business."* Jesus gave this model for us to follow. He will always be our example. He was always about the will of the Father. Every believer must be transformed into the likeness of Jesus and conformed to the will and plan of the Father for His Kingdom. Have hope and faith. You will discover your purpose as it flows through you. This week, reflect on God and what it means to be in the Father's house, taking care of kingdom business.

Reflection Questions:

- What does the will of the Father mean for you?

- What have been notable differences in your life when things just flowed?

- How passionate are you about fulfilling the will of God for your life?

Prayer:

Dear God, thank you for loving me and finding me when I was lost. Thank you for giving me Jesus as the best model and example I will ever need for life. Forgive me when I forget this or do not share the best of me. Please help me have a passion like Jesus for the Father's kingdom assignment, in Jesus' name, Amen.

Bearing Lasting Fruit for the Plan

Scripture:

You didn't choose me. I chose you. I appointed you to go and produce lasting fruit, so that the Father will give you whatever you ask for, using my name.

~ John 15:16 NLT

Woman of God:

God the Creator designed you. You are not a mistake or an afterthought for God. This scripture clearly says that God chose you. You did not select Him; He chose you first. This is a good verse to remind yourself of whenever you are feeling a little bit down or off balance. Not only did He choose you but the plan was for you to bear fruit. Not any fruit. Hear this: lasting fruit! In the fig tree story, it did not bear fruit. Jesus cursed it and the fig tree withered and died. Jesus just wanted a little fruit because He was hungry. But what use is a fruit-bearing tree that does not produce any fruit? For some, you may know what your fruit is and you are working diligently and wholeheartedly to produce good crops. Well done! Keep going.

For others, you may still be trying to discover what your fruit is and what you are supposed to do. That, too, is okay. You are still seeking. Well done. Just remember your fruit will last—whatever it is—for the benefit of others. Like teaching, evangelizing, being a worship leader, creating art or music, being a writer, and so much more. The fruit will impact others for the kingdom. You are the daughter of the Creator. You will have abundant fruit to share and to give. Remember that God does not make mistakes. He knows explicitly what He has called you to produce. So trust Him this week. Ask God—in Jesus' name—to help you visualize and reflect on your lasting fruit.

Reflection Questions:

- What are your thoughts on how your lasting fruit will impact others?

- Do you see your lasting fruit as an inheritance legacy?

- How do you feel about God choosing you to produce something lasting?

Prayer:

Dear God, thank you for drawing me closer to you each day and through these weeks. Thank you for my fruit that will last. Forgive me when I fret about life or what I cannot control, map out, or even understand. Please help me surrender that to you, and trust that you will complete what you have started, in Jesus' name, Amen.

God Grants Success

Scripture:

Commit your actions to the LORD, and your plans will succeed.

~ Proverbs 16:3 NLT

Woman of God:

The scripture tells you to commit your actions to God. Take a moment to grasp this. These actions refer to everything. From your troubles, cares, and emotions to new opportunities, ventures, and anything you hope to achieve. It further tells us that once presented to God, your plans will succeed. This should inspire you to keep God in the loop with all your concerns. He cannot help you if He is outside your plans; only from the inside. You may wonder why you need to commit everything to Him. You have the potential to affect and impact your relationship with God and change your life and the wider community. As you learn to entrust all things to God, you relinquish your self-control. You convey that you trust God and seek His counsel and guidance. Once you commit your way to God, He can guide and lead you in the way you should go for success. God is within you. Failing is not an option. God never created anything that fails. Failure is not your portion. Success is. Granted, you may try something that doesn't go right the first time. That's not failure. It's a learning curve. Perhaps there is more wisdom needed to do it better the next time. This week, reflect on how God wants you to commit your actions to Him so you can succeed.

Reflection Questions:

- Is it easy for you to relinquish your actions to God?
  If not, what might you do to change this?

- Knowing that God says success is for you, does this encourage you to move forward?

- What areas do you struggle to commit to God? Can you talk with Him about them?

Prayer:

Dear God, thank you for being you. Thank you for everything you created, which has a purpose and will succeed. Forgive me for the areas I am struggling in or with. Please help me see myself as you see me. Please help me share everything honestly and openly, knowing you love me, in Jesus' name, Amen.

God's Plan for Your Life

Scripture:

The LORD will work out his plans for my life—for
your faithful love, O LORD, endures forever.
Don't abandon me, for you made me.

~ Psalm 138:8 NLT

Woman of God:

Has it landed in your spirit yet? The God you serve will fulfill His purpose in your life. God cares about you so much. He also cares about what He has placed within you. These gifts and talents are distinctive to you and your assignment and they are for the benefit of others. Joseph had dreams. Solomon had wisdom. Perhaps you're a modern-day prophet. Or maybe it's education, nursing, housewife, caretaking, or songwriter. The list is endless. When thinking about this scripture, does it comfort you? It says God will complete His work. Look at His attribute here. It mentions His faithful love which endures forever. God will never stop loving you. That is so impossible as it lasts forever. So rest, Woman of God, and He will help you with the plan. He will fulfill His unique call on your life. God is faithful and true. He is a loving Father to you, His daughter and His child, and nothing can change this. Enquire of God if you are a little stuck on anything or unsure. He longs to hear from you and will come through for you. Let it settle in your spirit that you serve a mighty God who only wants the best for you. This week, reflect on God's faithful love that endures for you.

Reflection Questions:

- Have you settled in your spirit that God cares and wants your best? If not, what might you do here?

- Can you share your heart with God?

- Are you able to rest in God's loving assurances for you?

Prayer:

Dear God, thank you for knowing me more than I know myself. Thank you for your faithful love, which will endure forever. Forgive me when I cannot always see your love towards me or that you want the best for me. Please help me overcome this area so I will never miss your promises or goodness, in Jesus' name, Amen.

Testify of the Truth

Scripture:

But I will send you the Advocate—the Spirit of truth.
He will come to you from the Father
and will testify all about me.

~ John 15:26 NLT

Woman of God:

Being a follower of Jesus means you will testify of Him and the Good News of the Gospel at some point. Jesus came to free the captives from imprisonment. He opened your blind eyes and released you from a life captive in sin and darkness by sending one of His followers to testify to you. You, too, need to be sent to testify. However, it is not always easy. But praise God, the one who opens blind eyes to let in the light of the truth sent another to be with you, the Holy Spirit of God. The world is desperate for the good news, regardless of their blindness and misunderstanding. The Holy Spirit is the one who empowers you to step out and reach the lost and broken. Perhaps this could be the people where you work, or your friends, or even your next-door neighbour. Just know you will never be alone. You have the Holy Spirit of God residing within, strengthening you with boldness and courage to witness. The Holy Spirit will be beside you. Nothing will be impossible with Him. Seek counsel from God and ask Him who He would like you to speak to. Pray about it and be led to step out in expectant faith. Plant the seed. Others may reinforce the soil or add water but it will bloom in God's season. This week, reflect on how the Holy Spirit has led you to testify of Jesus to others.

Reflection Questions:

- Do you believe the Holy Spirit can empower you to do great things?

- How do you feel about the Good News of the Gospel?

- Can you share your faith and the Good News? If not, what prevents this?

Prayer:

Dear God, thank you for sending your Holy Spirit—the Advocate— to live inside me. Thank you for not leaving me alone; thank you for saving me. Please forgive me when I lack the courage to speak of Jesus, the Gospel, and my faith. Please help me surrender my will to the Holy Spirit so He can lead me wherever He wants, in Jesus' name, Amen.

The Father's Will

Scripture:

Then he said, "Look, I have come to do your will."
He cancels the first covenant in order
to put the second into effect.

~ Hebrews 10:9 NLT

Woman of God:

Congratulations, you have arrived at week 52! In the first section you saw the covenant-keeping God of the Old Testament. This scripture says God cancelled the first covenant to put the second one into effect. Jesus was the foreshadow of the old covenant. He came to do the will of the Father. He was the perfect sacrificial lamb, given once and for all for the forgiveness of sins. Jesus is the anointed High Priest who made it possible, by His body, to reconcile you to God through his death. The priests of old presented to God the blood sacrifice of animals to atone for their sins. Jesus became the perfect, sinless sacrifice in an act that only needed to be enacted once. Praise God for Jesus the High Priest. God wanted the new covenant written on humanity's heart not a stone tablet. God wanted it engraved on the conscious to convict and identify sin, whereby repentance and forgiveness would lead you back to God. The Holy Spirit living within you is the one who convicts you and prompts your spirit, changing you to become more like Jesus. God sent Jesus and He willingly came and fulfilled the Father's will. In this production of life you, too, have a role to play. You have people to impact, influence, share the gospel with, heal, transform, and love. The Holy Spirit will empower and equip you to do this with the love of God, move forward in humility, and serve others with good conduct and a just manner. Let your adventure begin and discover the will of the Father. Then serve wholeheartedly. He has arranged your purpose; you only need to walk in it. So, do not fret in the waiting. Live in expectation. Know that what God started in you, Woman of God. He will complete it. Now go forth and do His will.

Prayer:

Dear God, thank you for being with me in this 52-week devotional journey. Thank you for all your revelations and insight and for drawing me nearer to you. Thank you for keeping me close. Forgive me when I feel I do not have what it takes to be a sent one. Please help me know that I only need the Holy Spirit and a willing heart. Thank you that I can answer the call and impact lives for your Kingdom Glory. I love You. Please keep this flame of love within me ablaze and alive for you, in Jesus' name, Amen.

Afterword

Woman of God, well done for coming this far! I hope this devotional book has blessed you. I hope you have learned to foster new practices by finding a quiet place of reflection. And as you pray and seek God, your intimacy level has grown, taking your relationship to new heights. I know mine has. I pray that God will continually strengthen you to move toward God's plan and your heart's desires. If you feel in doubt, stuck, or going through a time of difficulty, revisit this devotional. God will reveal and expound new things to your heart as you do. Just remember He loves you very much and cares for you. Call upon Him anytime. He longs to hear from you. So, embrace this Holy God with all His wondrous attributes, which are too numerous to mention. But don't take my word on that. Spend time with God and see for yourself. Reflect on His word. Delight in God's promises to become all He created you to be to impact a world that is waiting for you.

Blessings,

Josephine Thomas

Author and Fellow Woman of God

About the Author

J osephine Thomas is a devoted wife, loving mother, and committed follower of Christ with a compassionate heart for serving others. Her dedication to ministry and charity work is evident in her unwavering support of widows, orphans, and the broken-hearted. Through her personal journey of navigating complex and painful relationships, Josephine has discovered the profound importance of building and maintaining a deep, significant relationship with God. She speaks from experience, having faced challenges that left scars on her tender spirit. Yet, in the Sacred Place of God's presence, she found healing, restoration, and the affirmation that God will never forsake, undermine, or devalue her. Josephine's testimony is one of triumph, as she learned to trust again and embrace her God-given purpose. Her passion is to see women healed, whole, and aligned with their divine calling—living lives that are fulfilled, joyous, and productive.

For information about group teaching or group coaching, please email: pureandunblemished@gmail.com

Website: www.pureandunblemished.com